Cinderella

Illustrated by Eric Kincaid

RED CIRCLE

Cinderella lived in a big house.
She was always busy. Her two
stepsisters made her work hard.
"Cinderella! Sweep the floor!"
"Cinderella! Wash the dishes!"
"Make the beds!"
"Clean the windows!"
Cinderella's work was never done.

Her stepsisters spent half the day
telling Cinderella what to do.
They spent the other half trying
to make themselves pretty.
"Cinderella!
Brush my hair!"
"Cinderella!
Tie my bow!"

"Powder my nose!"
"Fasten my buttons!"

One day a letter arrived at the house.

"There is to be a ball at the palace. We are invited!" shouted the stepsisters.

"Am I invited?" asked Cinderella.

"Even if you are, you cannot go," said her stepsisters. "You will be too busy getting us ready."

The day of the ball came. The
stepsisters kept Cinderella very
busy indeed. There was so much
to do. Poor Cinderella did not
know what to do first.

At last, the stepsisters had gone
and the house was quiet. Cinderella
sat by the fire and began to cry.
"If only I could
go to the ball,"
she wept.

"You SHALL go to the ball," said a voice behind her. Cinderella jumped up in surprise. She thought she was alone in the house.

"Who . . .who are you?" she gasped.

"I am your Fairy Godmother," said the stranger. "I have come to get you ready for the ball."

"Bring me a pumpkin,"
said the Fairy
Godmother. She
turned the pumpkin
into a coach.

"Bring me four
white mice," said
the Fairy Godmother.
She turned the
mice into four
white horses.

"Bring me three
lizards," said the
Fairy Godmother.
They became a
coach-driver and
two footmen.

"I cannot go to the ball dressed
in rags," said Cinderella sadly.

The Fairy Godmother waved her magic wand once more. Cinderella's rags turned into a beautiful ball-gown. Her bare feet were covered with dainty glass slippers.
"Now you are ready for the ball," said the Fairy Godmother.

"But first, a warning. You must leave before the clock strikes twelve. At twelve everything will change back again."

"I will remember," said Cinderella. "Thank you, dear Fairy Godmother."

Cinderella danced all night with the Prince. Her stepsisters saw her, but they did not know it was Cinderella. They thought she was a princess.

Cinderella was so happy she forgot all about the Fairy Godmother's warning. Then the palace clock began to strike the chimes of midnight. One . . . two . . . three . . . "I must go!" cried Cinderella and she ran from the palace.

"Stop! Stop!" cried the Prince.
Cinderella did not hear him. As
she ran down the palace steps she
lost one of her glass slippers.
... ten ... eleven ... TWELVE!!!

The beautiful gown turned into rags.
The coach turned into a pumpkin.
The mice and the lizards ran away.

The Prince found
her glass slipper
lying on the
palace steps.
He called to
a footman.

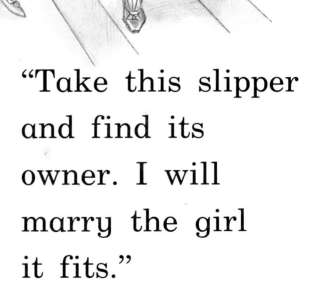

"Take this slipper
and find its
owner. I will
marry the girl
it fits."

The footman travelled all over the kingdom with the slipper. It fitted no one. At last he came to the house where Cinderella lived. "Let me try it!" said one of the stepsisters. She snatched the slipper from the footman. "Look!" she cried. "A perfect fit."

"No it is not!"
shouted the other
stepsister. "Your
heel is hanging
out. Give it to
me!" She snatched
the glass slipper.

It didn't fit her either, though
she tried to pretend that it did.
"Is there anyone else in the house
who should try the slipper?" asked
the footman.
"No!" said both stepsisters together.
"Yes there is," said their father.
"Cinderella has not tried it yet."

"The Prince would never marry HER!"
laughed the stepsisters.
"The Prince said everyone must try
the slipper," said the footman.
It fitted Cinderella perfectly.

Her stepsisters were so surprised
they fainted.

The stepsisters still looked
surprised when the Prince and
Cinderella were married.

All these appear in the pages of the story. Can you find them?

stepsisters

Cinderella

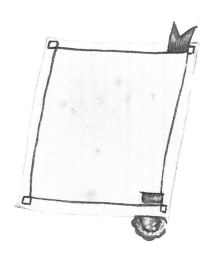

letter

Fairy Godmother